Is It Unforgivable

By K.L. Wheeler

I0115608

Text Copyright ©2016 K.L. Wheeler

Dedication

This book is being dedicated to the following:

God allowed a wonderful, beautiful, full-of -
life and funny lady to give birth to me. Peggie Jean
Jones-Clay, taught me how to love people, care for
them, as well as show kindness and mercy no matter
the situation. My life with her was not always easy,
but we had the most important ingredients in life:
God, Respect and Plenty of Love.

My Mom, My Hero.

My dear brother, Darryl Keith Clay, whose
life was taken at a young age. You were a little
brother, best friend, great uncle and a wonderful
father. You are missed dearly.

LaTanya Brown (Toni), who has a quiet spirit,
will help you out in a bind. I love you more than you
will ever know or understand. You have been there
through my entire life and I know that people really

3

read you wrong, but you have so much to give. Start giving away what God has given you and let go of the past hurts. God loves and cares for you. Keep God first and He will bring you through every situation.

My babies,

Antonio, Verneshia and Rodney. God gave me jewels when he gave me you. Thank you for supporting your mom and making her smile through some rough times. We have shared ups, downs, storms and life together.

Love y'all much.

Daddy,

You are missed dearly. Thank you for your love, kindness and allowing me to always be loved by you no matter what.

Thanks Daddy.

Acknowledgements

To my best friend and Savior whom without this book would not have come to light. God, you have watched me from my mother's womb to now. You have placed people in my life to be a blessing to me. I need you more than life itself. Please continue to direct me and guide me through my journey on earth. Thank you for the kindness, mercy and grace that you have bestowed upon me. I love you dearly, God the Father and Jesus the Savior.

My prayer partner and best friend, Vanessa Martin, has been with me from the beginning of my spiritual walk to now. I have shared many private and emotional moments with you. I thank God for giving you to me as a gift and I will always love you.

My godparents: Mr. Rufus Vester, Lena Vester and Carolyn Vaughn. Words are not able to describe what you mean to me. When I was confused, angry, lost, off track and just needed an ear, you were there. When my mom passed, you stepped in to fill the void. You have loved me through all of my mistakes and life errors that could not be corrected.

I Love Your Dearly

Candace Burton, nicknamed my P.R. person, I appreciate all your hard work to ensure this project was published, web based and on every genre that is currently out there. I can hear your VOICE, *Get to it Lenee*.

Love you Girl

Thanks to all my Zion Temple COGIC Family in Memphis, TN, my current pastor, Rosman Randle, and former pastor, Clarence Randle. Thanks for all of your support and prayers down through the years. You are my extended family. I have known you my entire life and this place of God was a great foundation for my spiritual life.

Kim

To all my family and friends, thanks for being there in your special way when I needed you the most. You know what you did for me. It could have been as much as read a chapter, listening to me talk about this project, computer help, support and words of encouragement. You did your part in this endeavor.

Table of Contents

Introduction

Growing from childhood to adulthood can be a rough and difficult transition. The road of life may not turn out the way you dreamt as a child.

A certain woman dreamed her life would consist of a wonderful man who would love only her as she would love him. They would grow stronger in their love and commitment together, marry, live in a beautiful home and have children. Her husband would work to provide for their family and as the wife, she would care for him while ensuring their children had a great upbringing and provide tranquility for the family. However, as she journeyed on the actual road of life, the dream became a nightmare. The picture became clear that her idea of life and reality were not on the same path.

As her life began to become nothing like the dream she once held so dear to her heart, the man she thought would bring her happiness, wholeness, and make her world complete, turned out to do just the opposite. She was introduced to heartache, turmoil and shattered dreams, a part of life that she was not prepared to handle. The nightmare was the beginning of her life lessons.

During her teenage years, the first sign of love entered her life. He was tall, dark, young and ever so handsome to her! They began a relationship which grew into her first love. She thought everything he did was adorable, cute and funny. From their passion, lack of knowledge, and experience, a child was conceived.

That is when she learns they, "the happy couple," were not as happy as she thought. The relationship began to fall apart. She found herself alone, pregnant and heartbroken. Where was her lover? The man of her dreams…left as if everything meant nothing. There were no more visits or phone conversations. It all ended in the blink of an eye. How could he do this to her and their unborn child? She had to deal with the disappointment that she saw in her mother's eyes: along with the harsh words that her father expressed about the situation she found herself in.

Everyone had words to express into her life which stirred her emotions of low self-esteem, anger, abandonment and the feeling of being without love; but, she began to suppress her feelings to focus on the baby and finishing high school. She endured the hardening effect of words, looks and her own self disappointments. Life moved on and the baby is born healthy and happy. Her lover began to come back around and she forgave him for leaving her to deal with the consequences and shame.

The relationship went back to what she thought was normal. They were together as father, mother and their first born son. Her dream began to come back to life and the couple was happy. The child grew and the relationship held together for a season. The mother went back to school focused on a career to support her son, while the father obtained employment to also support their son. As the relationship strained, the couple went their separate ways.

This teenage mother bore the pain of watching the man she loved and wanted to build a family with take their son around other girls playing house with several of them. Feeling like her boyfriend played out this phase, of course, she allowed him to come back to her. All in the name of what she thought was *love*.

Meanwhile, she graduated high school and landed a full-time job. They entertained plans for their future together as a couple. Of course, she was ready for marriage because she loved him, and only him. He, however, was not as focused on their future together as she is in her heart.

The young lady planned for her next move which was moving from her mother's house into a place of her own. The summer after graduation, on her 18th birthday, she moves into her first apartment. It was an upstairs unit with a living room, dining room, one bath and two bedrooms, furnished with only one bed and a 13" television. Boy was she happy to finally have a place to call her own and a sense of accomplishment.

Life was good again with love swirling around in the air. Of course, baby daddy visited and got interested in forming a life together. Happiness resurfaced once he moved in with them and their lives begin to flourish with things like furniture, a car and clothes. She saw her family as perfect, and dared anything or anyone to harm it.

After a couple of years passed, the baby started school, doing well. The lover of her life introduced her to a new level of pain. The one thing she thought no one else could have but her, he gave to another. A son was born from another relationship and her world shattered into pieces. She thought, *How could this be? How could he allow this to happen? What's wrong with me? Am I not pretty enough, slim enough, loving him enough and giving of myself to him?* Her love turned to hate. A side of him came to light that she never wanted to experience. How could she forgive him? The journey he had taken her on felt like an emotional roller-coaster.

Do you feel that something someone has done to you is an injustice and you just cannot seem to forgive? Is there hurt and pain that just will not seem to leave your heart?

This book, <u>Is it Unforgivable</u>, is referencing the book of Hosea from the Holy Bible (King James Version). Hosea was a man whose marriage God used to show His love toward Israel after they had departed from God, seeking other gods.

God spoke to Hosea and said:

Go, take unto thee a wife of whoredoms and children of whoredoms: for the land hath committed great whoredom departing from the Lord. Hosea 1:2

So Hosea did as God commanded him and married Gomer, a lady who was a harlot. She would leave to go lay with other men, and her husband would have to go and buy her back. He returned home with her after she had lain with other men. Much the same way God would take the children of Israel back after they went after other gods. They repeatedly hurt God by worshipping idol gods. They would forsake God and forget about all that He had delivered them from. Hosea allowed God to use him and his marriage to show Israel how much He loved them no matter what they had done. He forgave their transgression and accepted them back into a covent relationship.

God wants us to have a relationship with Him, so we should not allow anything or anyone to destroy our relationship with Him. Unforgiveness will destroy you and not allow love to have a perfect work in a relationship. God loved Israel so much that his mercy, longsuffering and grace allowed Him to take Israel back after they repented. God then healed them of their backsliding.

You will see that you *can* forgive and allow healing to work. There is nothing in this world that we can do to one another that is not unforgivable. God is our source for forgiveness in every matter. We have to learn how to show love toward the person that has wronged us.

Stage One

Dealing With Your Issues

We are all creatures who have several unresolved issues. Some of our problems can easily be dealt with. Then there are those we would like to leave in the closet, lock the door and throw away the key. Throwing the key away will not resolve what we know is lurking in our closets.

Gomer is known as the unfaithful wife of the prophet Hosea. During her time, under the Law of Moses, she was to be stoned to death for committing adultery. Hosea was given a commandment by God to marry her. The purpose of that union was to show Israel how much God loved them even after all of their whoremongoring with other gods. They had turned from God and created issues with themselves and looked for an outside source of comfort. An example would be in the case of Gomer.

When Gomer left her husband for her lovers, she was receiving something she thought she could only get from them. Every lover had a purpose in her life. Gomer may not have known that her husband was able to supply her needs. Maybe Hosea did not let her know that her needs and wants would be supplied by him.

There are several sources of our issues. Some stem from our childhood. Men and women may deal with the absent love of their fathers. We feel our parents did not give us enough things or love growing up. Men may be missing the masculine bond they need from their fathers. Hearing confirmation that their father would be proud of them, accepts and loves them as they are. In addition, we may have been teased or not accepted by our peers.

We are all looking for something or someone to fill voids in our lives. We never tell our parents how we feel and sadly, they may never ask us any questions. So, if no one communicates their feelings to each other either, no help is ever given to resolve these issues.

So how do you move on? Where are the answers to these problems? We may never know because the fear of being rejected is too much for us to bear. Parents do not have all the answers for us, because they sometimes do not understand themselves. Children do what they feel is fun at the time, unaware of the seeds they are planting. Their actions can have an adverse effect on their future. As we mature, we carry all of those unresolved issues into our adulthood. Eventually, all of the unresolved issues show themselves in different ways.

Men who were not approved by their fathers generally learn to show no outward emotions displaying tough exteriors where they build high walls. Some never let go of their fathers' absences which in turn affects their relationships with their children and wives.

Women who have unresolved issues will tend to act out their emotions with unhealthy relationships. They have relations with men who are just like their father or worse. They need the love of a man to fulfill them where their fathers did not provide that love. For some, food is known as the comfort that will not let you down. For others, shopping soothes the lonely hearts and of course many turn to the fairy tale love stories watched on television. Then there are times we act out to have our way and in return, we hurt the people who love us. We do not want anyone to get close in fear of betrayal, disappointment or rejection.

We must learn to slow down, retreat to a quiet place and evaluate our lives. Ask yourself, "Why do I act this way? What is really bothering me? Do I love me the way that I am? What makes me do the things I do?" Only when you deal with your own issues will you be able to heal and ask God to help you along this tough road of recovery.

We have cause and effect in our lives that result in our behavior. Dig deep to uncover what is causing your problems and then you can change the affect it has on your life. Ask God to search your heart, then help you to deal with yourself. He can heal and deliver you from your issues.

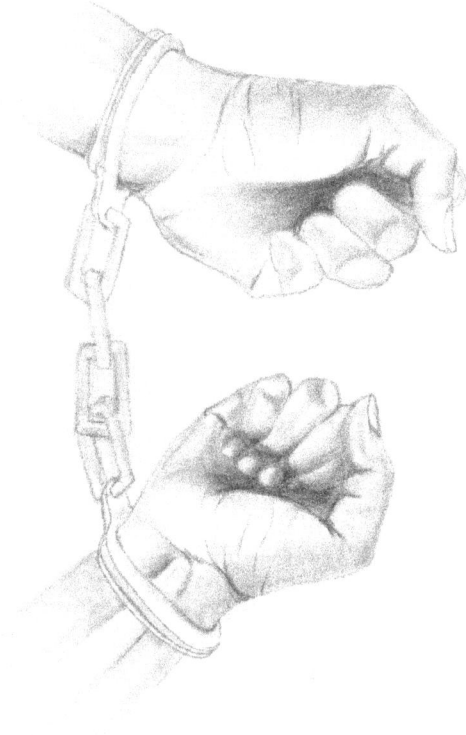

Stage Two

The Prisoner Is You

When you think of a prisoner in our society, you may think of someone locked in a correctional facility or prison. Most prisoners have committed some type of crime; however, there are a few prisoners incarcerated as scapegoats for crimes they did not commit. There are others who have committed no wrong, but were found guilty of a crime.

The prisoner who committed the crime has to deal with his or her punishment. Some feel that the punishment does not fit the crime. The scapegoat feels like he has been wronged in some way and should not have a punishment. The prisoner who has done no wrong feels that an injustice has been committed toward him or her and they should be able to walk away and be given some type of restitution such as a public apology, fresh start or money for their pain and suffering. All prisoners have the right to feel their way. Now, we will examine each prisoner.

The prisoner who is actually guilty has to deal with his/her conscience. They may analyze the why's of what brought them to this point in their lives. Some may go back to childhood to find what went wrong and why. *Where does the fault lie? Am I really the person they say I am? Did I do all of what I was found guilty of?* They may also feel as though they are the victims after having time to think about their lives and what has happened to destroy it.

The prisoner who is the scapegoat now realizes that his/her friends have left them alone to deal with the situation. No matter how exciting or fun the act may have been, they are now left alone. They wonder where is the group they had on the outside, all of the buddies, road dogs and so called friends. Unfortunately, they understand that they have been left to do the time alone because being the scapegoat does not really pay off. They might become angry with themselves or the groups that helped get them there. The scapegoat wants to tell the truth, but no one wants to hear it.

The prisoner who is truly innocent continues to spend his time trying to convince others that he should not be in prison. He did not do the crime he was found guilty of. People will not listen to him/her because they have heard that same sob story so much that they have become numb. This prisoner hears things in his head like:

> I don't belong here.
>
> I did not do it.
>
> I am innocent, it is true.

The innocent spends all his time in prison trying to prove he/she does not belong there.

Now that you have looked at the prisoners of our society, focus on the prisoner we carry around with us every day. The person who cannot forgive is holding themselves prisoner. You are holding yourself captive every day, when you say, "I cannot forgive them for what they did to me. I was hurt and they ruined my life. Do you see that your mind is holding you imprisoned every day? How can one thing in life ruin the rest of your life? Never allow anyone to have that much control over your life. No one situation can ruin your entire life, unless you allow it to enslave you. There is one key that can help you walk out of your prison and *you* hold it! Take the key of forgiveness and walk out of your prison… take a deep breath and let it all go! Start today walking in a newness of life that you have never felt. Set your mind, heart and spirit free of all issues.

Philippians 2:5, Let this mind be in you, which was also in Christ Jesus.

Once a prisoner has been set free, they are given a second chance at life. Now is your opportunity to have a second chance, go ahead and take it.

A child once analyzed the rain and windshield wipers on a car. The child inquired of his parents, "Do you see how the rain is coming down and how the wipers keep wiping it away?" The parent answers, "Yes." The child said, "That is how God does us. We sin, we ask God for forgiveness and God wipes it away."

Children are some of the most forgiving people in this world. We must learn to be just as forgiving as God and little children. Let's look at the rain story a little further. Once the rain is gone, the clouds pass away and the sun begins to shine again. That is the beauty in forgiveness. You can shine again! Once you have asked for forgiveness, God will give you a pardon, and then the wall between the relationships will be torn down. This is also true with all relationships. Unforgiveness puts us into a prison with walls.

This is the time to start building new things in your life. This is the opportunity to build a new you, better relationships and better days. Become the person who you can live with and be happy with each day. The road ahead looks much brighter and more beautiful. See it! Obtain it! Believe it, and start walking in it!

Unstable

The Bible tells us this in James 1:6-8;

But let him ask in faith, nothing wavering. For he that wavereth is like a wave of the sea driven with the wind and tossed. For let not that man think that he shall receive any thing of the Lord. A double minded man is unstable in all his ways.

There are several things in life that are predictably unstable. Cars can be unstable due to maintenance issues. If homes are sitting on a cracked foundation, they become unstable to live in. The economy is unstable. Jobs are unstable. Everything in this world can be unstable at one time or another. God wants you to believe in Him, so that your life will be stable.

Your mind is like the steering wheel in a car; it controls your body. If your emotions become unstable, you are considered unstable. You may begin crying for no apparent reason, or act out emotionally toward people who have not done anything to you to deserve that type of behavior. You may even feel withdrawn from people because you do not trust them with the intimate details of your life. The enemy uses this has a weapon against you. Your decision making skills are inhibited when your emotions are unstable. Your vision for the future turns bleak deterring your ability to trust our own instincts.

When you became a teenager, you were told that your hormones were out of control. The boys would act different from the girls, most notably the voice deepening from a soprano to more of a baritone. Girls on the other hand, start crying and yelling when things do not go their way. Dads feel helpless because they were losing their little girls to womanhood. Moms would like for the house to stay together. So the whole house experiences years of hormonal changes.

Compared to our spiritual stability, there will be several trials that will almost knock you off your feet or make you feel like you are losing your mind. There was a time in my life that I had three deaths in two months. My mom was the first loss which was devastating. My stepfather passed 30 days after my mother. Then the death of a 20-plus-year relationship, called my marriage. Each of which had its own emotional responsibility.

When mom passed, I had this feeling of emptiness because we had grown to have a friendship beyond just a mother-daughter relationship. My stepfather had been in our lives since I was a little girl, so it was very much like a father passing away and the final blow was the death of my marriage. I believe that was the blow that began my emotional rollercoaster. I had feelings of failure because I had put so much of *me* into this marriage. I felt this was a personal failure that *I* caused. I experienced feelings of low self-esteem. During these times, I asked the question, "Why me?" These are circumstances that cause your emotions to become unstable.

You must learn to recognize what is going on with you before you can begin to know how to attack it. Your mind is the place where all thoughts are conceived before the body acts them out. When your emotions are on attack, so is your spirit. The enemy is after your soul and that is his ultimate goal in your life. He does not care what he has to do to get it. Our spirit must be stable at all times. We need God to keep our spirit in tune with His spirit. When you are unbalanced in your emotions, you will act childlike; doing what feels good to you without thinking about the consequences.

The Bible tells us:

1 Peter 1:13, Wherefore gird up the loins of your mind, be sober, and hope to the end for the grace that is to be brought unto you at the revelation of Jesus Christ.

We believe in everything, but we always want to try God last. We believe that are cars will crank; our jobs will always be there; we will wake up in the morning and life will continue. But try this way, believe in God for everything that life brings you and see that your outcome will be better. We should learn to ask God for His wisdom in our lives so that we will be able to make better decisions. Then, we will not become so unstable. We must seek God and ask Him to stabilize us in every situation. Learn how to get your emotions under control and believe God. With His direction, you will not to waiver.

God is our helper in time of trouble. Learn how to lean on Him when life's storms are knocking at your door and you feel overwhelmed. His word tells us that we are in his hand and no man is able to pluck us out.

Pray this prayer, *Lord and Father give me stability in my emotions, mind and spirit. This will help me to serve you better and to have a clearer outlook on the situation. In the name of Jesus I pray, Amen.*

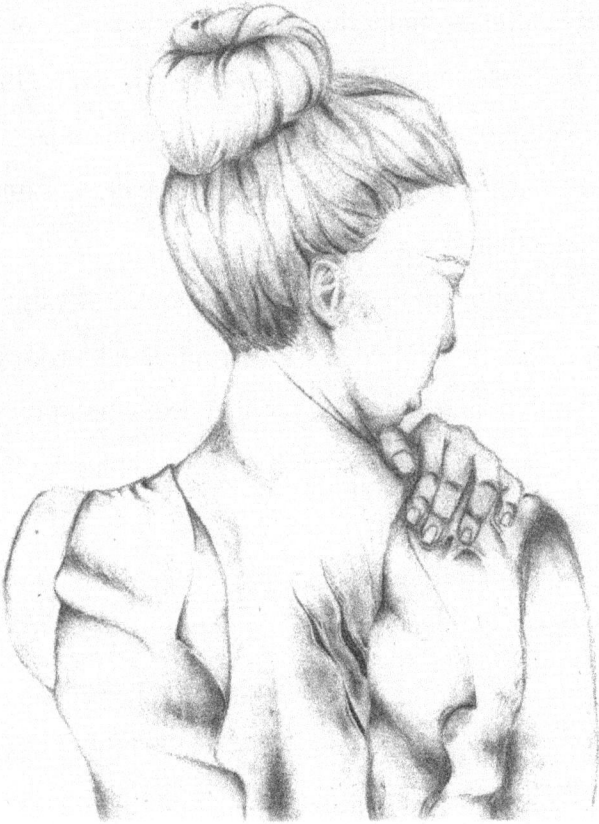

Stage Four

Covering Up To Mess Up

You are taught to cover situations up, never dealing with them or destroy the hold they have on you. Regardless of how ugly situations may appear, you still must learn to uncover them and deal with solutions. This is a tool that the enemy uses to keep you in bondage.

I remember while attending high school, my grades fell below average (ex: D's or F's). Since I was enrolled in a typing class, I would use the typewriter to white out the bad grades replacing them with better grades (ex. A's or B's). I covered up the bad grades for six weeks. The only problem with this plan was, I had to remember to do it every six weeks when report cards were issued. *What would happen when I forgot to cover up the bad grade?*

Now, here comes the part that was the mess. I had to answer to my mom about my grades. Mom was disappointed in me and I had to own up to my bad grades. It was time to tell mom about my short comings in the classes where my grades had fallen. I had to change my approach in that class and study more, listen to the teacher and do my homework. When you cover up the mess in your life, you are unaware of the ugly stain that is produced behind the scene.

Forgiveness and unforgiveness work the same way, if you never forgive yourself, a person or a situation, it will only leave an ugly stain in your heart. When your heart is not right, it keeps you from God's true love.

Your heart and mind are like memory banks. Over time, you store information about events that have happened during the course of your life regardless of whether or not the events are good or bad. Unforgiveness leaves an ugly stain in your memory bank and that deposit only comes up to keep you feeling angry, hurt, depressed, lonely and guilty to keep you down.

It is now time to forgive and use the experience as a stepping tool to move higher. Forgiveness releases you from feelings of anger, guilt and shame allowing you to move away from the past.

Forgiveness will help you to love again and see the world in a whole different light.

Take a look at another example of covering up. Say a family has a beautiful new house recently built. As you walk through, you notice the plush carpet, beautiful kitchen cabinets, clean bathrooms and large closets. Everything in this new house is clean, new, no scars, neat and beautiful. They purchase new items such as a stove, refrigerator, washer, dryer, pictures, beds, drapes, tables and all the accessories for a house.

The family of six moves in making the house a home. They settle into their new surroundings. Everyone begins to migrate to their rooms. The family celebrates this milestone in their lives. Now, fast forward to this same family twenty years later. The children are all grown and have moved out. Mom and dad begin looking for a smaller home for the two of them. They find a beautiful, cozy house and decide to move.

The parents have made wonderful memories in their old home. The time finally comes to start packing and moving. Therefore, when the furniture begins to be moved out of the house, they begin to see the rug, walls and floors again. They are able to notice the wear and tear of the home such as the holes, dirt, scars and trash that were not visible before. The furniture covered the mess for years, but now the family has to clean and scrub to get the house ready for a new family. Once the cleaning has been done, the home is beautiful again.

It is the same way with forgiveness. If you do not forgive, you put furniture, pictures and decorations up to cover the blemishes in the home rather than cleaning them up. You cover up the beautiful, loving person God has created from those trials with His own hands. Once you forgive everyone, including yourself, you will notice the scars leaving and God will clean your temple and His light will shine again. Loving is so much easier than hating.

Uncover whatever is not right and deal with the situation. Only when you are true to yourself, can you begin to grow and love the person you are. Once you love yourself, you can show love to others.

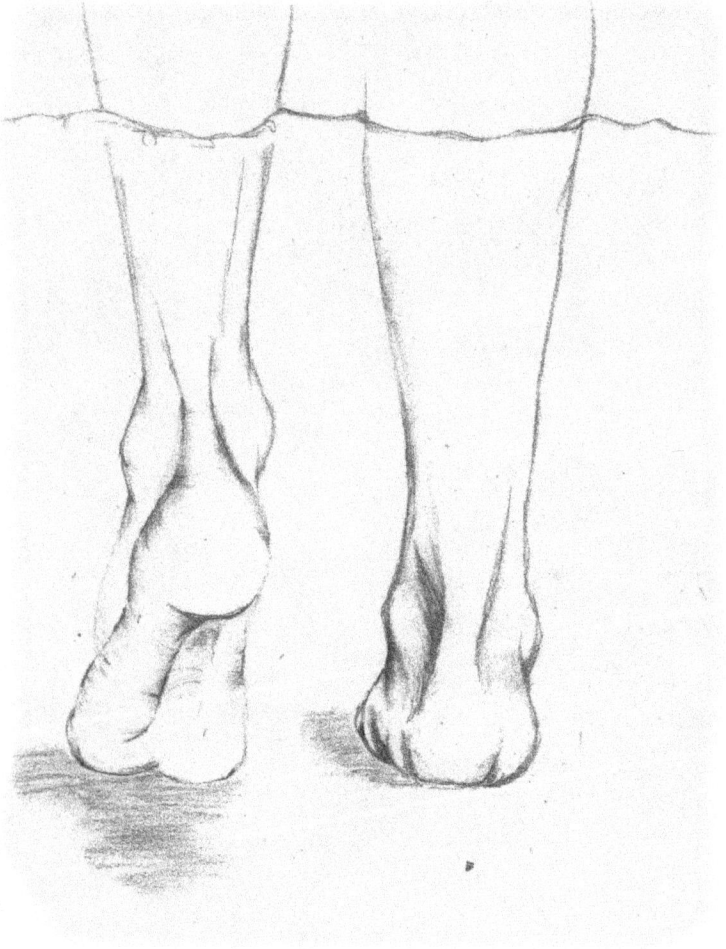

Stage Five

The Damage After The Storm

A natural storm comes in different ways and can strike at any time. There may be warning, while at other times they come unexpectedly. Clouds appear, thunder roars, lightning flashes, hail or rain plummets to the ground. Storms can last a few moments, but have lasting effects with damages that take time to repair.

After the storm passes, you must look back to assess the damages. Some of the damages may be property and some may be emotional. You are able to deal with the property damage pretty easily, but the emotional damage may take some time. You call your family and friends and inform them that everyone is okay. Then, you must contact your insurance company to file a claim for damages. You prepare your family to move to a more stable environment if necessary, and gather what you can salvage. As you go back to visit the damaged area, you begin to realize what this storm has taken from you and your family. You may shed some tears over the items and possessions, such as your home clothes, car, family photos and memories, but the one thing that is still standing would be YOU! Step back and see that God has left you here for a reason; a reason that He will fulfill.

Just like there are natural storms, we experience spiritual storms as well. I see this as a time when you are driving on the highway and you run into a rain storm. You pray God will allow the rain to let up and bring you through. It may get heavy and force you to pull over on the side of the road, but something in you tells you that you can make it. You begin to allow the fear to disappear and strength comes giving you the courage you need to keep going. Then you look in the rearview mirror to see that the storm is now behind you, and you can see clearly in front of you.

Spiritual storms are not always as easy to see, like the natural. We really never see it has a spiritual attachment until we are in the midst of it, or when it is completely over. If you have decided to give your life completely to God, the enemy is headed your way with many storms. The Bible states in

John 10:10, **The thief cometh not, but for to steal, and to kill, and to destroy: I am come that they might have life, and that they might have it more abundantly.**

Our lives will have spiritual storms that will rock our world as we know it. If you realize that what is happening is a storm, you will learn how to fight back with your spiritual weapons.

Once in my life, there was a storm that was threatening to take me down mentally. God spoke to me and said, "You have put all your concern on this situation, I need you to direct yourself toward me." I begin to shut myself up in my home and started seeking God in a way that I had never done before. I gave God my weekends and gave up everything else (ex: shopping, talking on the phone, running in the streets); I also gave up my bed and moved to sleeping on the den floor. I locked myself in the room with my Bible and spiritual CDs. God began to minister to me until I took my focus off the situation and put it on Him.

I allowed this storm to take over my every thought. When I begin to see what this was doing to me spiritually, God gave me a way out. This storm took away my self-esteem, leaving me feeling empty, depressed and rethinking a decision that I had made earlier in life.

A spiritual storm can have the same effect on you as a natural storm. It can come through and destroy everything that God has put in you. Then, as you take a look, you can see what damages have been done. You may go through this type of storm for years before you open your spiritual eyes to see what has happened. You are left with a feeling of unworthiness, helplessness, emptiness and low self-esteem. There is a feeling of being unloved and being friendless among so many other feelings that tear you down instead of building you up. This is when you will realize totally what has happened to you. You should immediately seek help from God to rebuild your life.

God is the only source that can rebuild you after this type of storm has torn down everything.

There are spiritual storms that are necessary to uproot some of the generational attachments such as alcoholism, promiscuity, disobedience and adultery embedded deep in our souls. This will allow God to pluck and prune the unfruitful things out of your soul.

In a natural storm, some trees are uprooted from the ground, as there are some things in our heart and soul that need to be displaced. Many may come from when we were a child. One of these things could be unforgiveness. This is a seed that is planted in children at a tender young age. You hold on to things that may have happened to your parents or yourself as a young person. You could be harboring this emotion, having never allowed it to be torn down in our hearts.

Learn to recognize the different storms that come your way. Ask God to give you a spirit of discernment to clearly understand what is being attacked. As we mature, we learn what the good things are to hold on to, and what things we need to release. Some of the houses that were destroyed in those storms I spoke of earlier did not have a good foundation.

So as with your spiritual life, you should be concerned with building a solid foundation. Therefore, when a storm comes you are able to weather through and make it safely on the other side. As each storm comes, you should always take a learning experience away with you. Look back in your life and see what has been damaged, then ask God to rebuild you from where you are today.

Stage Six

Forgiving Yourself

The problem with forgiving yourself is that you are with *you* all the time and are able to remember what you have done. You are constantly thinking about your life and the wrongs you have done to yourself and others. You can feel the pain of your wrong doings, trying to convince yourself that things will get better. You reason within yourself about whether or not you need to talk to someone else about the situation, only to find they really cannot help.

The exact same issue can resonate with people differently. You must remember that God is your strength, source, and the ultimate problem solver. You can tell God everything! He knows and understands your pain and sorrow. God knows and understands you better than anyone, including yourself.

There is no one but God who you should totally put confidence and trust in. God is the only judge who can judge all things perfectly. The bible tells us to put no confidence in the flesh and that would include you.

Psalm 118:8, It is better to trust in the Lord than to put confidence in man.

I have learned that forgiving yourself is harder than forgiving others. This is an inside problem that no one can see but you and God. Unforgiveness leaks into your heart and begins planting and growing seeds of discouragement, shame and depression. You will no longer have the strength or desire to go on with life. You begin to pull away from friends and family telling yourself that you want to be alone to get things together. Your life seems to be falling apart and you do not know where it begins or when this feeling will subside. Your decisions send you on a rollercoaster ride; only when you confess your wrong and seek God will this ride stop.

This act may seem like it is impossible. I have had to struggle with forgiving myself of my sins. Once you know to do better and you still do not behave yourself, it is hard to say those acts were a mistake. You have all too well learned the difference between good and evil. Then the enemy tells you that God will not forgive you because you knew better or because you have done this before and you really did not mean to do it again.

You experience feelings of unworthiness because you have hurt God. Questions plague your mind: *Does God hear me? Will He answer me? Did I mess this relationship up? Is it over with Him? Has He given up on ME? Will these feelings ever leave me?* You pray, then feel God has not answered you. You seek out people who may understand your situation and have a solution to your problem. It is also perfectly normal to feel isolated from everyone or that no one knows how you are feeling. All hope in everything is lost, discouragement sets in making it difficult for you to even move on.

But there is a little part of you that says God will forgive me and hear my cry. You plead with God to forgive you and now you must be willing to forgive yourself. Whatever sins have been committed, you must learn to live with yourself and your decisions.

Come clean with God and pour your heart out to Him. Once you reveal it, He can heal it.

You have to take ownership of your wrong doings, because once they have been done, there is no taking them back.

The enemy tricks us into believing that no one will be hurt by our actions, but the truth is you are hurting yourself in ways you do not see or understand right now. Ask God to help you not to fall into the enemy's traps. Pray for the ability to discern the times and fully understand what God is doing in your life. This might seem like an impossible task, but you can overcome. Philippians 4:13 states: I can do all things through Christ which strength me. It is imperative to ask God for the strength to overcome self.

There is good reason to forgive you. The whole process of forgiving has to do with believing that God has the power and desire to forgive you. Just like you trust God when forgiving others, you must trust Him when forgiving yourself.

God already knew the things you would face before you were born; therefore, failures are no surprise to God. They are a surprise to you. Yes, we all have fallen short of God's Glory; you are no exception to the rule. No matter how much you give, do for others or try to be good, you still have to ask the Father (God) in Jesus' name to forgive you and heal you to possess the ability to forgive yourself. The same freeing power you feel when you forgive others, you can expect to have that power when you forgive yourself.

One reason why people have such difficulty in forgiving themselves is due to the relationship/covenant that we have entered into with God. God is our Father and no child wants to disappoint their father. Children always want the approval of their father; they never want to do anything to destroy that relationship. This fellowship is more precious than any fellowship in the world. The shame and hurt comes in when you betray this relationship. You cannot talk to your father like you once did because you know, as well as He, what you have done. Fear comes in and you no longer want to talk to your father because of your sin. You are concerned that others will know how bad you messed up with Him. How can you move where God wants you to be if your own unforgiveness is holding you hostage? In order to forgive others, you must be able to forgive yourself.

The sins you have committed should be punishable by death, but the governor has called a stay at the final hour and given you a pardon. A pardon for a prisoner can only be given by the governor of that state. When a pardon is given, it means excusing an offense without penalty. To allow an offense to pass without punishment. This is what Jesus does for us before God,

I John 2:1-2 states: My Little children, these things write I unto you, that ye sin not and if any man sin, we have an advocate with the Father, Jesus Christ the righteous; And he is propitiation for our sins; and not for ours, only, but also for the sins of the whole world.

When you forgive yourself, you release the guilt and shame of your actions. Then hope replaces guilt and shame because when you forgive you release those emotions and pick up to live again.

The bible says in Romans 5:5:

Hope maketh not ashamed; because the love of God is shed abroad in our hearts by the Holy Ghost which is given unto us.

Hope offers you a positive outlook on things to get better with a spirit of expectation of being fulfilled. You have confidence that God will make you and your situation better. There is only good in forgiving yourself. You begin to see things differently and want to help others see their situation is not hopeless. This does not have to take your life, hope and love from you. But take up your bed and walk in Jesus Christ (John 5:9).

Jesus frees you and lifts all the weights of sin that you may be free in Him to do all things. It is time to take the covers off you, tear down every wall, get out of bed, and put on your helmet of salvation to protect your mind and heart.

You must feed your mind the right things to hear and know your direction. Your shield of faith is knowing that God will help you every step of the way giving you strength to beat the enemy and all his fiery darts. Your feet shod with the preparation of the gospel of peace. There must be peace in forgiving which is the word of God. Now that you have dressed yourself with the proper attire to live life, you are able to forgive others and God is able to forgive you. This is a time when your father's love shines because He loves you so much He has open arms ready and waiting to forgive you. That is how love works. Even though He knew you would sin against Him, He still loves you with an everlasting love. He's not there to continue to remind you of how bad you are, but He wants to restore you back to fellowship with Him.

A loving father is always ready to welcome his child back home, as in the parable of the Prodigal Son. No one wants their sins spread out for everyone to see or hear about. Instead of trying to understand, people will just judge and speak without knowledge of all the facts. No matter whom you are or what you have done, all anybody wants is to be loved and accepted.

Allow God to *over*shadow you with His love so that you may be healed and restored back to Him. You must believe that He has forgiven you; walk in forgiveness and **LIVE!!!**

Stage Seven

Release Hurt

Hurt means to afflict with physical pain; to cause anguish to; to feel or be a source of pain.

In this definition, we see several ways to be hurt. You should be able to identify with physical pain from childhood to adulthood; at some point or another, you have physically hurt at your own hands or the hands of someone else. Physical hurt heals; the healing process is visible. Sometimes the wound is aggravated which causes it to re-open takes longer to heal.

The second definition is "to cause anguish to," which means extreme pain or distress to the body or mind. Let's discuss hurt of the mind. This type of hurt is much harder to heal than physical hurt. When hurt attacks the mind, it can become deadly if not dealt with properly. We must recognize that it is there and then – as soon as you recognize the attack – you can begin to deal with it. When your mind has been disturbed, your whole being is disturbed. You have to readjust so everything will fall in place correctly.

Isaiah 26:3; Thou wilt keep him in perfect peace whose mind is stayed on thee: because he trusted in thee.

This is why you cannot allow hurt to dwell in your mind. Hurt can take away your peace. As you meditate on it, you can become more affected or infected by it. The more you dwell on the situation, the more it can affect you and your actions.

Another form of hurt is when you become the source of the pain. There are different ways that you can be the source. When you are the person inflicting the pain or you do not release the hurt, you are able to stop inflicting the hurt once you recognize the point of origin. Maybe you hurt people because you have always been hurt. Therefore, you will not allow yourself to trust people and you hurt them before they have an opportunity to hurt you. Maybe there has never been a true friend in your life to show you love despite your faults. Whatever the case, you are now the source of your hurt and you must deal with it.

When you choose not to release the hurt, you have become your own prisoner. The hurt comes out in various ways: actions, words and decisions based on your pain. You are like a wounded animal. When animals are hurt, they protect the wound, separate themselves and hide out until the wound is healed. They will not allow you to touch them without trying to protect themselves instinctively.

People are sometimes like those wounded animals when acting on our emotions. We hide out with sleep, food, TV and whatever it takes to keep away from the hurt. This does not heal the wound; it just suppresses the pain until we deal with the problem.

Proverbs 18:21A: Death and life are in the power of the Tongue.

St. Matthew 12:37: For by thy words thou shalt be justified and by thy words thou shalt be condemned.

Our speech allows hurt to stay alive. The way you continue to talk about the hurt in a negative way keeps the pain alive. You have to change the way you speak about your hurts. Learn to speak with power and victory, instead of, resentment and pain in such a way that it becomes a testimony of how you have overcome with the victory. Thank God for the lesson. Your life can be an inspiration to help someone else.

Decisions should not be based on your pass hurts. Allow yourself to trust again because you can shut down all new possibilities from new friends and jobs to relationships. Why? Because past hurts that you have not healed from can ruin your life in the present. Now is the time to get the best of the situation and stop letting it get the best of YOU!

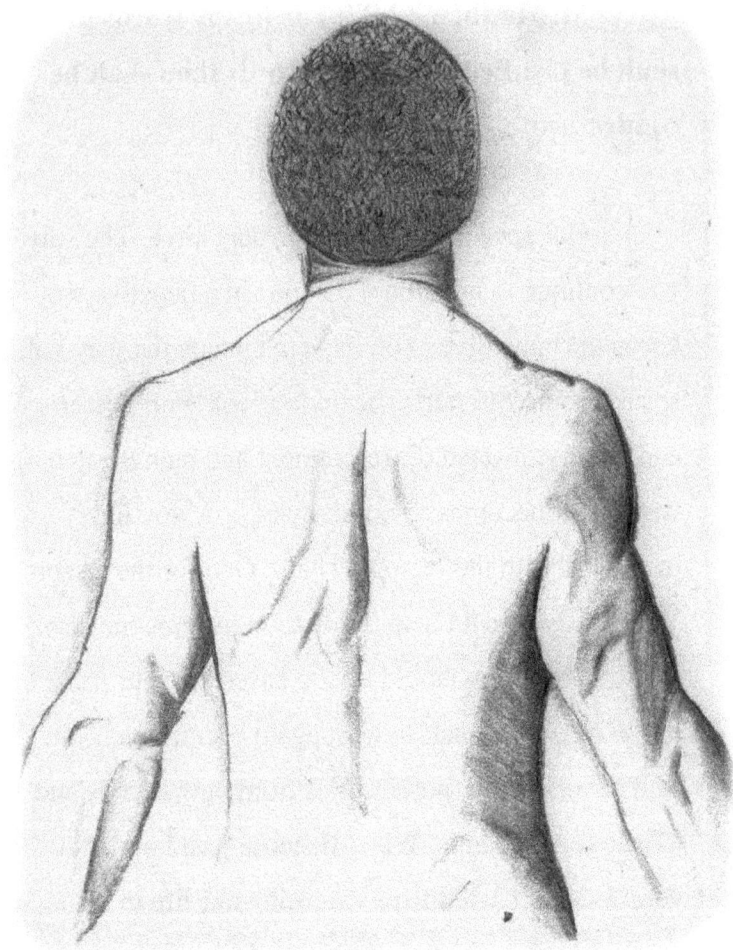

Stage Eight

Feel Healing

Jeremiah 30:17: For I will restore Health unto thee, and I will heal thee of thy wounds saith the Lord; because they called thee an Outcast, saying, This is Zion, whom no man seeketh after.

Healing is a process that takes time and energy. In order to have healing, there must first be a wound that caused hurt. When you have been wounded, you naturally shut everything and everyone out to protect yourself. You no longer allow life, love or freedom to have a part of you. When one has been hurt, we try to understand and cover up the pain. In order to feel healing, we must open the wound, clean it out, and apply bandages for a short time before removing the bandages for healing to begin.

Wounds sometimes may go a long period of time before we acknowledge that there is something wrong. Ignoring the wound allows time for it to develop an infestation of your body or on your Spirit.

61

Recognizing the wound does not belong wherever it appears takes great strength and forces you to seek help beyond yourself. This may lead to seeking professional or spiritual direction and learning how to move forward to resolve the situation.

One of the treatment suggestions may be to perform a surgery or allow God to cut out the negative in your life.

Surgery is sometimes a necessary process to remove or correct something that is affecting the whole body. The definition of surgery reads as *a branch of medicine concerned with the correction of physical defects and the repair and healing of injuries and the treatment of diseased conditions especially by operations.* Surgery is a last resort after all other ways of resolving the illness has been exhausted.

Once the surgery is completed, you move from the operating table to a place called the recovery room. In recovery, you are still sedated from the anesthesia administered to you before the surgery. Anesthesia causes you to lose bodily sensation with or without loss of consciousness. More often than not, the anesthesia is responsible for the loss of consciousness that makes you lie motionless and unaware of your surroundings. Once the medication wears off you become alert again. If there are no complications you are released to go home to start your healing process.

When you allow the hurt or pain of a situation to stay in your life, your healing cannot begin. Just like surgery, you must allow God to come in and remove what is affecting the whole body. We will not go through life without hurt, so we must allow God the chance to heal our mind, body and soul. God is our healer. We must give ourselves time with God alone to be still and motionless, so that his Spirit can minister to our hurts and wounds.

It is the same as when the doctor tells you to go home, stay off your feet and get plenty of rest. The reason you cannot go back to the normal way of life, is due to the healing process. Why not give God the same time that you would give a doctor who has performed surgery on your body. Your spirit needs time to get away from everyone and everything to receive healing from God. Do not look at your surroundings, situations or spoken words to re-infect your wounds with germs of negativity. Listen to the Spirit of God, and once His Spirit has ministered to you, the hurt will be released and healing will begin. Healing is a great and wonderful emotion. You can return to your life, take the bandages off, show your scars and began to love again!

Jesus says in Matthew 6:14-15

For if ye forgive men their trespasses, your heavenly Father will also forgive you: But if ye forgive not men their trespasses, neither will your Father forgive your trespasses.

Do not allow your hurt to keep you in bondage. Free yourself by forgiving and living again.

Stage Nine

The Bottom Is Not The End

When learning how to swim, you start at the lowest level of water and work your way to the deeper water. Once you have become a good swimmer, you are able to go to deeper water and test your skills. One thing you learn about deep water is that once your feet touch the bottom you must use them to get back to the top. You use your feet to push your way up to the top of the water. Similarly, when life hurls curve balls to hurt you, you must push yourself back up. You have to conquer fear, depression, anger and resentment to rise again.

God says in Isaiah 43:25:

I, even I, am he that blotteth out thy transgressions for mine own sake, and will not remember thy sins.

If God lets go, and does not remember the sin that we have done against Him, we must also do the same when people have sinned against us. Dwelling on what has been done in the past will not help you to let go or heal you. What if God dwelled on your sins before He blessed us? He might not continue to bless you!

Hanging on to thoughts of your sins would only remind God of how you hurt Him. Whereas the devil keeps you in a regressive mindset focusing on past hurt and disappointments, God forgives through mercy, longsuffering and love.

Learn from Jesus and do the same thing to your fellow brothers and sisters. It is time to forget the cliché that says: I'll forgive you, but I will never forget. The time is now to forget and move on with your life.

Micah 7:19: He will turn again he will have compassion upon us: he will subdue our iniquities and thou wilt cast all their sins into the depths of the sea.

Start casting into the sea, by having compassion for one another and forget. Allowing the thought of what people may say when you forgive the worst in others should not rule your decision to let go. Clutching on keeps you at the bottom of the situation, weighing on your heart and spirit.

It has been spoken that you are at the bottom. Realize who spoke those words, was it God or satan? Satan's words are temporary and speak death, but God's words are permanent and bring life. Jesus says in John 10:10:

The thief (satan) cometh not, but for to steal, and to kill, and to destroy: I (Jesus) am come that they might have life, and that they might have it more abundantly.

The bottom is not the end! For some people, it is just the opposite. This is now their beginning! They have been stripped of all the things they thought were important in life, leaving them time to listen and hear from God. In listening, they find out that He is what they needed to value most in this life instead of the things and people that take focus off God. The way we go about obtaining trivial things and building negative relationships causes a downward spiral. Lying, stealing, deceiving, scamming, cheating and all kind of other ungodly things cast you further away from God like a rock settle to the bottom of the ocean.

Unforgiveness can make your life sink to the bottom and cause you to never rise. It sets a root of bitterness and anger in your soul that eats away at your Spirit and cause you to die. To forgive is to live. There is a sin that God will not forgive in Matthew 12:31-32:

Wherefore I say unto you, All manner of sin and blasphemy shall be forgiven unto men; but the blasphemy against the Holy Ghost shall not be forgiven unto men. And whosoever speaketh a word against the Son of man, it shall be forgiven him; but whosoever speaketh against the Holy Ghost, it shall not be forgiven him, neither in this world, neither in the world to come.

Is It Unforgivable   K.L. Wheeler

If God is willing to forgive you for all the things you have done to hurt Him, what is holding you from forgiving others? Is not God much greater than you? Who are you to say that you cannot forgive? What is so bad that you will not offer forgiveness? Pray to God for a repenting and forgiving spirit to help you in our daily walk with Him.

You have to stop categorizing things according to society's view as being unforgivable. Actions as lying, adultery, murder, and homosexuality are promoted as unforgivable. Even children who have disappointed their parents are deemed unforgivable. Whatever society endorses as the worst thing that can possibly be done is said to be forgivable. You have done things to God that you are ashamed of and would never want anyone to know. So, stop being so critical of others and start helping them heal through forgiveness. You can rise from the bottom and see the top again. Praise God!

Stage Ten

When The One You Trust Betrays You

What do you do when the one you trust betrays you? This question may not be easy to answer, due to unresolved issues that come with betrayal. Betrayal has more than one definition. Here are a few:

- **To lead astray; deceive;**
- **to disappoint the hopes or expectations of;**
- **be disloyal to; to be unfaithful in guarding, maintaining, or fulfilling;**
- **to reveal or disclose in violation of confidence: to betray a secret.**

Trust is something that you initially give freely. When you meet someone for the first time, the first thing that comes to mind is not distrust. Examples can be the repair person who knocks at your door; the mail man who delivers your daily mail;

your hair stylist; the children's day care or school; your coworkers; your pastor; the doctor and our neighbors. There are several people who you trust without a second thought.

Everyone has a person in high school who they considered to be their best friend and would almost give their lives for each other. You tell each other secrets and maintain this bond that no one should come between you. You marry the love of your life, and believe they would never do anything to make you feel like someone has ripped your heart out of your chest and stomped all over it.

You put hope in a company that you have given 20 years of commitment. There's the idea of true leadership that you believe in keeping you as a loyal employee. When these relationships fall apart, you begin to feel as though no one can be trusted. So you give up hope of ever allowing yourself to trust anyone or anything again.

Women are some of the most trusting creatures there are. They trust everyone and never give it a second thought. Men, on the other hand, are reluctant to just open themselves up to trust everyone they meet. Most men are not as willing to just give you another chance, but women may allow you back in their lives. Women give husbands several chances to get their acts together before they call it quits. Parents give their children multiple times to correct there wrongs after they have trusted them to do the right things and the children failed. Friends do not just separate after the first storm comes to test their friendship, they work through the storm.

So how do you think your heavenly Father feels about you? He tells you He is long suffering, not willing that any should perish. He allows you to mess up 10, 20, 30 or more years of your life; even through that time you still may be hesitant calling on Him.

The problem comes when you open your heart and give so much of yourself to a person and they treat it casually. Or they share your deepest fears and personal opinions that you have shared with them with others. They commit acts against you that you thought they would never do. This throws you off your feet. *Not this person, how could they? I trusted them with everything.*

Those are usually the words that come after a betrayal. You first try to understand how the offense could have happened. *Why would they do such a thing to ME?* You go over every detail of your relationship with this person and you wonder what went wrong. Betrayal like this is hard to overcome, but is not impossible. You feel that if this person could do this, then who can you trust? You find truth to the saying, "No man is an Island to himself."

Without a doubt, you do need others in your life. There is no reason that we could ever understand why a person would betray us.

Look back in your own life and see where there were times when you, yourself may have betrayed someone. Maybe it was something that you considered small at the time, but now that it has happened to you, the picture becomes clearer. The smallest of things can make a person feel like you have betrayed them:

- not showing up on time for an important event in their life
- not returning a phone call at a crucial time for someone
- not taking out time to show that you really cared

Emotions are so fragile that sometimes the smallest of things can hurt us. Betrayal is an act that can be forgiven and restitution can come to the relationship. There is a scripture that states"

"My soul, wait thou only upon God; for my expectation is from him," Proverbs 62:5.

Quite possibly, you have placed unrealistic expectations on the people in your life. They may not even be aware of what you expect from them if you never communicate what you want or how you feel when that need is not met.

If you release people from your expectations, you will not feel betrayed when someone does not come through as expected. You put hope in an imperfect person making yourself subject to betrayal in one form or another at some time in your life. Teach yourself how to wait on God to guide you through relationships.

Look at Jesus as a perfect example. Judas betrayed Him and look at what it cost him. Judas went and hung himself. Just like you feel terrible when you are betrayed. Think about the person who committed the betrayal. They probably feel worst and may find themselves thinking, "How could I do this to my friend? Will they ever forgive me? I know that I have truly messed up this time."

Then think to yourself, if you could offer those three little words, "I forgive You?" Well, Jesus did it on the cross. He said, "Father, forgive them for they know not what they do." Maybe the person is unaware of what your friendship really means to them or how much they really mean to you. Maybe this mistake will help them to realize their error and make them want to change. You are the person who could allow their healing to begin, then watch God create a beautiful new creature.

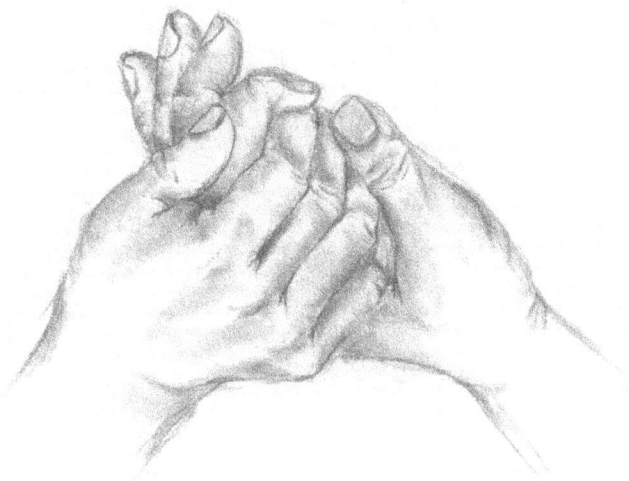

Stage Eleven

Then said Jesus, Father, forgive them; for they know not what they do. And they parted his raiment, and cast lots. Luke 23:34

Will everyone who has wronged you ask for forgiveness? No, you must forgive even when you are not asked. Jesus asked God to forgive the people who were crucifying Him because they were unaware of whom it was they were doing this wrong to. Jesus was also asking God to forgive us. We are the reason that Jesus went to the cross. Sin is what brought our Savior from Heaven to be crucified on the cross. There will be times when people are unaware of the wrong they are doing to you and you must forgive them.

Forgiveness releases you from captivity and helps you to heal. This one act will help you in ways that you may never understand. Look at it from this point: When you allow yourself to forgive someone, it releases all those feelings of anger, hatred and bitterness that have attached themselves to your heart.

Matthew 15:18 says: But those things which proceed out of the mouth came forth from the heart and they defile the man.

When you do not release forgiveness, you allow sinful feelings to set up in your heart and ultimately have the potential to defile your temple (body). The whole body will go to ruin because you have allowed a germ to enter your heart. The word germ is defined as a small mass of living substances capable of developing into an organism or one of its parts. Notice the word small in this definition. You allow *small* things to build into mountains. The more you focus on a situation the larger it becomes.

When you allow a germ to carry on the activities of reminding you of your hurt or the person who inflicted you with the pain, it grows into an organism. Organisms are dependent on something or someone to live. You must bind unforgiveness and kill it at the root. There is no survival in the present or future if you keep reliving a situation over and over again. Kill the germ so that it will not turn into an organism which needs your attention and focus to remain living.

Remember, society has certain crimes that it considers to be among the worst. A few examples are:

Murder	Incest
Adultery	Molesting
Lying	Treason
Rape	Prostitution
Whoremongers	Robbery
Disobedient Children	
Crimes against Children and Elders	

The list could go on forever. When someone has committed one of these acts, the feeling is that it is unforgivable. God does not agree, He says that all sin and iniquity is forgivable.

One of the disciples inquired of Jesus how many times must he forgive his brother. Jesus replied seventy times seven. No one person will offend you that many times. This does not mean you will not feel the pain; it just lets you know not to hold onto the pain. Forgive the person, not so much for them, but for your own self. You need to be free of the burden to move on with your life.

I am not saying that this should go unlooked. I'm just stating that they are not acts of unforgivable sins such that you should allow to dictate the rest of your life.

Adulterers and whoremongers, in our society, are looked upon as terrible people, not worthy of forgiveness.

Marriage is honourable in all, and the bed undefiled: but whoremongers and adulterers God will judge. Hebrews 13:4

Most of these acts will be known by the two parties and God alone. In today's world, we see the person who commits adultery as the bad person; however, I have learned that sometimes you can actually be the one who causes your own pain. Take inventory of your relationships to see if you are the one who is defrauding them. Defraud means to cheat, fraud, to take from, swindle. There are times when we take our love from the person we are supposed to give it to.

Let the husband render unto the wife due benevolence: and likewise also the wife unto the husband. The wife hath not power of her own body, but the husband: and likewise also the husband hath not power of his own body but the wife. Defraud ye not one the other, except it be with consent for a time, that ye may give yourselves to fasting and prayer: and come together again, that Satan tempt you not for you incontinency. I Corinthians 7:3-5

Once the act has been committed, you cannot wish it away. It has been done and the time has come for you to deal with it, just like you must learn a lesson from every situation that happens in your life. The problem that you fear is that the worst experience has a lesson to be learned. Look closely at the events that has happen and see what is beneficial from this incident to help you in your future.

Most acts that are committed against you cannot be taken back. If your loved one is murdered, that life will not be given back. If your spouse commits adultery, part of his spirit has been given away to another. Disobedient children cannot take away the heartaches they give. Friends and family are not able to take away the hurt they bestow on you. No act is reversible, but forgiveness is the only thing that can help you move forward with life. For those people who have wronged you, go ahead and forgive them; release your heart to be free of that burden.

Murder is a subject that I would like to talk about for a moment. This act may be inflicted by a person with no emotions or no remorse. What comes to mind is the remembrance of my brother's murder when his son asked, "Why did they kill my dad?" I still have not been able to answer that question as of today. My first emotion was clear…revenge. I wanted to strike back.

When a life is taken, there is nothing that anyone can give you that will replace the true meaning of what that loved one meant to you and your family. There is an emptiness left in your heart that you just cannot seem to fill. Two families have been affected by this terrible tragedy; the victim's and the accused's. The victim's family is angry and upset with the other family, and the accused's family may not have an idea of what the victim's family is feeling. The victim's family is not concerned about the accused family's feelings.

Two families drawn together by one terrible act. The victim's family has to come to terms that their loved one is gone forever. And there is a judicial system that will never render fair justice in their eyes.

We, the victim's family, had to endure hearing horrible things about my brother during the trial process. The family was asked to hold all emotional outbursts and wait patiently for our turn to address the court. The process of court delays and a trial weighed heavily on my family's emotions. We had to come face to face with the accused and never take any actions against them for what they had done. We had to listen to lawyers go through a lot of legalism defending someone they did not know or love.

That whole process can leave you angry, resentful and depressed. The accused may never ask my family to forgive them. With prayer, during the proceedings, and time spent with God helped me offer them my forgiveness. Through this entire ordeal God was able to help me to forgive the accused. I forgave them and moved on with my life.

I learned that holding on to all of those emotions did not help me to heal from the loss of my beloved brother. Nothing that neither I, nor the judicial system could do would give me my brother's life back.

Ask God to help deliver you from anger, resentment and depression because it could always be you on the other side inflicting pain.

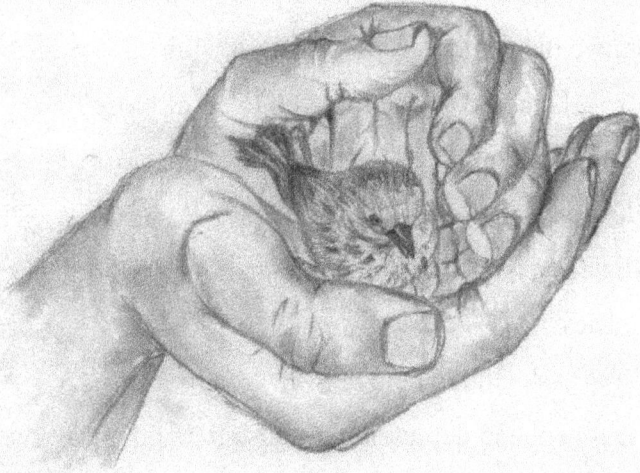

Stage Twelve

A Person Knows When They Are Forgiven

A good example of forgiveness is the story of Joseph, Israel's son in the book of Genesis from the Holy Bible. Joseph was seventeen when his problems began. He was yet innocent, pure and full of life. Expectations and life had no limits for him. If we begin with Chapter 37 in the book of Genesis, it tells us that Joseph was just out feeding the flocks with his brothers and he heard them talking evil.

He reported all to their father. Israel loved Joseph more than any of his other children because he was the son of his old age. This was the first problem which Joseph had nothing to do with. He was the youngest child of an old father. His brothers recognized this and hated him because he was his father's favorite. His family hated him for something he had no control over. They would not speak to him in a peaceable matter.

When Joseph started dreaming and revealing his dreams to his brothers, this made them hate him even more. Also his father began to rebuke him when he told his dreams. In all his dreams, his family bowed down to him.

Then his brothers began to envy him, however, his father observed the sayings of Joseph. Joseph did not give a thought to the fact that his life was ruining the lives of the people around him. He was excited about the dreams and how his life was going. Then one day his father sent him out to look for his brothers. His brothers saw him coming from afar off and conspired against him to kill him. They said to themselves, "Let us kill him and then see what comes of his dreams."

There was one brother that spoke up for him and did not want to kill him. There was an agreement made to sell him into slavery. Joseph was taken from the family that he loved, but who did not love him. His captivity placed him in a strange land with strange people. But God planned for his life to be this way. He prospered in every area of his life.

Joseph and his brothers reencountered each other in Egypt during the famine. Joseph had years to understand and speak to God about how his brothers separated him from his family at a young age. Joseph learned that his life was a plan from God to save his people from death. Joseph was glad to be reunited with his brothers and father after so many years of being apart. He told his brothers not to be grieved or angry with themselves for sending him to Egypt for God sent him to preserve life. Joseph removed everyone from the room and was alone with his brothers. He broke down and cried when he was reunited with his brothers. He kissed them on their necks and this was done in a private reunion, but afterwards everyone heard about how glad Joseph's heart was to be reunited with his brothers.

His separation was to help many people live through years of famine and lack. Joseph had a wonderful spirit and did not hold on to their injustice in his heart. There were several people who blamed Joseph for things that he did not do. But each time he was blamed, he never revealed that it was someone else.

Joseph showed true forgiveness for the wrong that was done to him by people who were supposed to love him. He accepted the path that was given him and was able to save his entire family. He humbled himself and released the anger and was forgiving even when they never acknowledged their wrong toward him. God, in return elevated Joseph to the position of Governor for Pharaoh in Egypt.

When God forgives, you will feel his genuine love, kindness and mercy. God does not hold back his love, even remembering how we have hurt him. The same should be true when you forgive others. The person should feel the genuineness of your forgiveness knowing that you are no longer harboring any ill feelings toward them.

Forgiveness is a small act, yet reaps a great harvest. Israel's family was put back together, where they were able to find love and trust. They multiplied and prospered.

Allow yourself to forgive with no ill feelings toward anyone. Observed the growth in your spirit, your natural life and the freedom you will have to love.

Stage Thirteen

The Journey

We are all on a journey called life. During this journey, everyone encounters successes and failures. My journey has been one of multiple successes and more failures than I would prefer to tell you about.

As a little girl, I had high hopes and dreams for my life. You see, the journey of life offers a great opportunity to explore the whole world, but as you mature you see the ugly side of this great world. It is nothing like you imagine in your dreams. There are obstacles in this world that you may overcome, and there are some that may overtake you.

My mom never told me that I could not do anything and the world gave me a picture of never achieving my dreams. My first obstacle in life was having a baby as a teenager which was a very interesting adventure during the early 80's. Giving birth to this bundle of joy did not seem like such a wonderful event. The normal things you would think someone would know about having a baby, were not so obvious to me. I was looked upon as a fast-tailed little girl.

In reality, I was a scared little 14-year-old. I had no clue how my life was about to change and there was no one willing to give me an insight on the big change ahead. Well, he came and all seemed to work out. However, having a little guidance would have been so helpful.

In your journey, there are many things that people will not be willing to discuss with you, as if somehow not discussing these issues will make them go away. Well, they do not go away. You just make very unwise decisions and those choices cause greater obstacles.

I went on to discover that going to college was another rock in my life that I would have to climb alone. So, I went to work to care for my baby boy. Under educated with a baby out of wedlock was beginning to have a heavy load on a very young lady. This made me think about the decisions I had made.

You have family and friends who are on your journey should give you help, but we really don't talk about what is really bothering us or what we are really dealing with. There are so many emotions s that are held in and never released. People go through the whole day asking, "How are you?" without stopping to wait on the response. I really think asking is just a formality and no one cares to hear the answer.

This journey has taught me so many things and if I could go back in time, I would change some of them. I do realize what has happened to me has made me the person I am today. Mastering the art of listening could very well lead to fewer failures on your journey.

There was a time in my life when people around me warned that I would need God, but I just thought they were old and did not know what they were talking about. I gave my life to God at the tender age of 13. However, there was no form of learning for children of that age group in the church to understand what this new relationship really meant. My desire was to live for God with all I knew. My heart was yet pure and undefiled. I was excited about this decision and wanted nothing but to do his will.

Is It Unforgivable   K.L. Wheeler

Do you remember me saying that people do not like to discuss what is going on in their lives? Well, this was one of them. I did not understand that I needed to read the Bible to learn about this new relationship with God, so in my little mind, I went back to being a little girl and gave into the world that was around me.

God is a much needed person on this journey of life. I have made many mistakes, regrets, failures and successes, but I truly believe that things would have been better if I had God from the very first step. I believe that God is with us from our mother's womb. There does come a time when we have to make a decision to keep God in our lives.

Usually, the times He is needed the most are the times you exclude Him from the journey thinking you can conquer this whole world with the little knowledge you have obtained. Once I realized that my life had a big missing piece of the puzzle, I soon started to search for it. God is the best thing that has ever happened to me on my journey.

Trust is given away so easily to people in your life, yet you have a hard time giving everything to the one you should trust the most. Even after learning that I needed God, I still made mistakes and bad decisions on my own. I had to learn that I have someone in my life that loves me more than I love myself. He knows what is best for me in the end. I had to come to a realization that God is not some fairy tale, but He is the wonderful, loving Father who has been there from the beginning, and is always there to help on this journey.

God will not leave you; it is the other way around. You allow the enemy to plant this seed in your heart that God does not want to have anything to do with you. God loves you; He just hates the sin that is in you.

As a child, I thought that God was this big, mean man who, as soon as I did something wrong, was there with a baseball bat ready to get rid of me. As I began to build my relationship with Him, I learned that he was crazy about me. I was made in his image. There are many things that I wish I could take back in my life, but the truth of the matter is, I cannot. So come what may, **I am my journey**.

You must learn from the journey that you have created, and take the good with the bad. Make the road ahead better for yourself and those around you. Learn to speak to one another and listen with a pure heart, without any prejudices. It is comforting to speak out and just have someone to listen.

Trust me when you mess up, you are harder on yourself than anyone could ever be. You do not know or have all the answers to life issues, but I truly believe that God will take you through this journey and make it a better road if you just trust in Him with all your heart.

Laurel Rose Publishing

Laurel Rose Publishing is an independent publishing company located in North Mississippi. The company was created as a way for unknown authors to get published and get help in marketing their works. If you are interested in publishing a book and want to know how you can do so contact us at www.laurelrosepublishing.com.